GREAT
COMEBACK
CHAMPIONS

Bo JACKSON

Super Athlete

Written and Illustrated by Jim Spence

THE ROURKE PRESS, INC.
VERO BEACH, FL 32964

D1555713

Edited by Sandra A. Robinson and Pamela J.P. Schroeder

LIBRARY OF CONGRESS CATALOGING-IN-PUBLICATION DATA

Spence, Jim
    Bo Jackson, super athlete / written and illustrated by Jim Spence.
        p. cm. — (Great comeback champions)
    Summary: A biography of the man who overcame a childhood of poverty to become one of the great stars of professional baseball and football.
    ISBN 1-57103-006-9
    1. Jackson, Bo. 1962-   —Juvenile literature. 2. Baseball players—United States—Biography—Juvenile literature. 3. Football players—United States—Biography—Juvenile literature. [1. Jackson, Bo. 1962-   . 2. Baseball players. 3. Football players. 4. Afro-Americans—Biography.] I. Title. II. Series: Spence, Jim. Great comeback champions.
GV865.J28S64   1995
796.332'092—dc20
[B]   95-5358
                                           CIP
                                           AC

Printed in the USA

Crack! The sound of the bat echoes throughout the stadium. "It's a long fly ball. It's way out of here—a home run! Bo Jackson is the most amazing athlete I've ever seen!" shouts the TV announcer.

3

Starting Out

As a child in Bessemer, Alabama, Edward Jackson often found himself getting into trouble.

"Hey, who stole my lunch?" cried Edward's classmate. While the teacher went to help the boy, young Edward sneaked outside with the missing lunch in his hands.

Bo came from a large family that did not have much money. Bo loved his mother, but missed having a father at home. "We never seemed to have enough food to eat so I would often steal other kids' lunches. What I needed was a father's love, and a father to teach me right from wrong."

Turning It Around

Bo's mother often prayed for him, but he still got into trouble. She got so worried, she was ready to send him to reform school.

When Bo saw how serious she was, he decided to change. He realized how lucky he was to have a mother who loved him and believed deeply in God. Bo began to use all of his energy in sports.

During his years at McAdory High School, Bo Jackson did very well in several sports. On the track team, he broke the state record in the 100-yard dash. He was also the state decathlon champion two years in a row.

    On the football team, Bo was the star running
back. He had gained 1,173 yards and scored
17 touchdowns in a single season. He was amazing
in baseball, too. He hit 20 home runs in one season,
breaking the school record.

Going to College

Bo's fantastic athletic records made the New York Yankee baseball team take notice. They offered him a multi-year contract when he was still a senior in high school.

However, Bo's heart was set on going to college. In 1982, he went to Auburn University in Alabama and began to break all of Auburn's rushing records in football. With Bo Jackson in the backfield, the Auburn Tiger football team beat the Alabama Crimson Tide for the first time in 10 years.

Everyone at the university was excited that Bo was playing for Auburn. He was also on their track team and played baseball, batting .401 and smashing 17 home runs in one season.

At the 1984 Sugar Bowl game, Bo Jackson ran for 130 yards to help Auburn defeat Michigan, 9-7. Many people compared him to the great Jim Thorpe, who was a great football and baseball player in the early 1900s.

Bo ended his college career by winning the Heisman Trophy—an award given to the most outstanding college football player in the United States.

At 6 feet, 1 inch and 225 pounds, Bo was an outstanding athlete who could do well in almost any sport. Many professional football teams wanted Bo to play for them, but he shocked everyone by choosing professional baseball instead.

Turning Pro

The Kansas City Royals picked Bo in the 1986 baseball draft. His first major league home run was a 475-foot blast—probably the longest ball ever hit at Royals Stadium.

Bo also had great speed and a powerful throwing arm. Time after time he drew crowds to their feet, as he caught balls way over his head, or outran a throw to first base.

In 1987, Bo Jackson decided to play professional football. He wanted to play football in the fall for the Los Angeles Raiders, and baseball in the spring with Kansas City. Many people thought this was a bad idea. They thought Bo would not have the strength to play both sports. Bo proved everyone wrong. He broke the Raiders' rushing record by running 221 yards in a single game.

Fighting Back

Bo was so good that he made the all-star teams in both baseball and football. He became famous and appeared in several television commercials. Before long, everyone around the world knew the expression "Bo knows ..."

On January 13, 1991, Bo was tackled during a football game and suffered a hip injury. The doctors told him he should stop playing sports.

Bo knew he could never play the rough sport of football again, but hoped that someday he could return to the baseball diamond.

Bo decided to have surgery to get an artificial hip. His new hip worked well and he came back to play baseball. He went to play for the California Angels and started once again to chase down fly balls and hit home runs.

"Bo Jackson is a hero to me," says Kansas City Royals baseball great, George Brett. "When he's playing his best, it's a sight to see. It is beyond your wildest dreams!"

Bo

JACKSON

TIMELINE AND TRIUMPHS

1962   Born November 30 in Bessemer, Alabama

1981-82   Became school decathlon champion two years
in a row on McAdory High School track team

1982   Set high school record in baseball—20 home
runs in only 25 games

1982   Gained 1,173 yards in 108 carries and scored
17 touchdowns on high school football team

1983   Sugar Bowl Game. Voted Most Valuable Player

1984   Liberty Bowl Game. Voted Most Valuable Player

1985   Won Heisman Trophy

1985 Best single-season performance (1,786 yards), Auburn University football team

1985 .401 batting average, 17 home runs, 43 runs batted in, Auburn University baseball team

1986 Chosen first overall in the National Football League draft

1989 Voted Major League Baseball All-Star Most Valuable Player

1990 Voted to the National Football League All-Star Team

GREAT COMEBACK CHAMPIONS

ARTHUR ASHE
Tennis Legend

BO JACKSON
Super Athlete

JOE MONTANA
The Comeback Kid

JULIE KRONE
Fearless Jockey

MUHAMMAD ALI
The Greatest

NANCY KERRIGAN
Courageous Skater